CONTENTS

THE ROMAN WORLD

The Romans were a very superstitious people, and they worshipped many gods and goddesses. Most of their gods and myths were based on Greek beliefs. However, the Romans gave the gods their own names.

TEMPLES AND WORSHIP

The Romans built many temples dedicated to their gods. Roman people would pray at these temples. They would also leave presents to encourage the gods to hear their prayers. Sometimes, the Romans would visit a special priest or priestess, called an oracle, to learn what would happen in the future. As the Roman empire grew, many foreign gods and myths became popular. The Persian god Mithras was worshipped by Roman soldiers because they felt he could give life after death to those who had died bravely in battle.

AT HOME

Romans believed that there were guardian spirits that dwelled in their homes and protected them. Most Romans had their own small shrine in their homes where they could pray every day. They would leave offerings of wine, cakes and spices.

Faunus was the god of shepherds who also told the future. He had the head and chest of a man, and the legs of a goat.

GRAPHIC MYTHS

ROMAN MYTHS

by David West

illustrated by Ross Watton

BOOK HOUSE

0129910682

Designed and produced by
David West 🖈 Children's Books
7 Princeton Court
55 Felsham Road
London SW15 1AZ

Editor: Kate Newport

Photo credits:
Page 4/5 (middle), Buckaroo
Page 5 (bottom), mlane
Page 6 (top), Sue Colvil and Bart Parren

First published in 2006 by **Book House**,
an imprint of **The Salariya Book Company Ltd**
25 Marlborough Place, Brighton, BN1 1UB

Please visit the Salariya Book Company at:
www.salariya.com

HB ISBN 1 905087 77 2
PB ISBN 1 905087 78 0

Visit our website at **www.book-house.co.uk**
for free electronic versions of:
You Wouldn't Want to Be an Egyptian Mummy!
You Wouldn't Want to Be a Roman Gladiator!
Avoid joining Shackleton's Polar Expedition!

A catalogue record for this book is available from the British Library.

Printed on paper from sustainable forests.

Manufactured in China.

ROMAN NAMES:	GREEK NAMES:
Jupiter	Zeus
Juno	Hera
Minerva	Athena
Pluto	Hades
Neptune	Poseidon
Bacchus	Dionysus
Diana	Diana
Venus	Aphrodite
Apollo	Apollo
Ceres	Demeter
Mars	Ares
Vulcan	Hephaestus
Cupid	Eros
Mercury	Hermes

Roman temples like this one in Sicily were copies of much older Greek temples.

Neptune was the brother of Jupiter, the king of the gods. Jupiter gave Neptune the sea as his kingdom.

The main guardian spirit was the Genius. He was worshipped by everyone, including the slaves. There were also Lares, who protected the household, and Penates, who looked after the store cupboard and all the food and drink in it. There were also State Lares who protected the Roman nation and were celebrated in public ceremonies. The emperor was seen as the State Genius or guardian, and many emperors were worshipped as gods when they died.

THREE ROMAN MYTHS

Although many Roman myths are based on older Greek myths, there are some that did originate in Rome. The three stories in this book are all original Roman myths.

Ancient Romans believed that Rome was built by Romulus.

AENEAS' JOURNEY

The Romans believed their empire was started by a Trojan hero named Aeneas. It is the story of an epic journey to find a new home for the defeated people of Troy. Aeneas was the son of Anchises, a human, and Venus, the goddess of love, and because of this many of the gods offered him help on his journey.

Aeneas
A Trojan hero. The son of Venus and Anchises.

Anchises
The mortal father of Aeneas.

Apollo
The god of the sun, healing and music.

Dido
The queen of Carthage, North Africa.

Lavinia
The daughter of King Latinus who marries Aeneas.

The Sibyl
A prophetess who lives in a cave at Cumae, Italy.

Turnus
King of the Rutulians.

Venus
The goddess of love and mother of Aeneas.

ROMULUS AND REMUS

The name Rome comes from the most famous of all Roman myths, the story of Romulus and Remus. It tells the story of the twins' early lives and the founding and building of the city of Rome.

Amulius
The jealous brother of Numitor.

Numitor
The ruler of Alba Longa and grand-father to the twins.

Rhea Silvia
The daughter of Numitor and mother of Romulus and Remus.

Remus
The twin brother of Romulus.

Romulus
The twin brother of Remus and the founder of Rome.

HERO HORATIUS

The Romans loved stories of heroic deeds. The story of Horatius Cocles has been shown in paintings and poems ever since early Roman times. Long ago, the people of Rome were under attack from many tribes. One day a huge army of Etruscans attacked Rome, and all that stood between the invaders and the people of Rome, was Horatius and his brave defence of the bridge over the River Tiber.

Horatius Cocles
The Roman soldier who defends a bridge against the Etruscans.

Spurius Lartius
A Roman soldier who helps Horatius defend the bridge.

Titus Herminius
Another Roman soldier who helps Horatius defend the bridge.

THE WANDERINGS OF AENEAS
(ANCESTOR OF THE ROMANS)

AFTER NINE YEARS, THE SIEGE OF TROY HAD STILL NOT BROKEN. WHILE DEFENDING THE CITY, AENEAS IS WOUNDED BY DIOMEDES. AENEAS' MOTHER, THE GODDESS VENUS, RUSHES TO HELP HIM...

SWOOSHHH

OH, NO!!! MY SON, MY SON!

APOLLO, THE GOD OF HEALING, SEES THE DANGER THEY ARE IN.

VENUS AND AENEAS ARE WOUNDED!

APOLLO SHIELDS THEM FROM THE FLYING ARROWS.

AS HE LEADS THEM AWAY, APOLLO LEAVES BEHIND A COPY OF AENEAS TO TRICK HIS GREEK ENEMIES.

IN THE TEMPLE OF APOLLO, ARTEMIS AND LETO HEAL AENEAS OF HIS WOUNDS.

SOON, AENEAS IS STRONG ENOUGH TO CONTINUE FIGHTING.

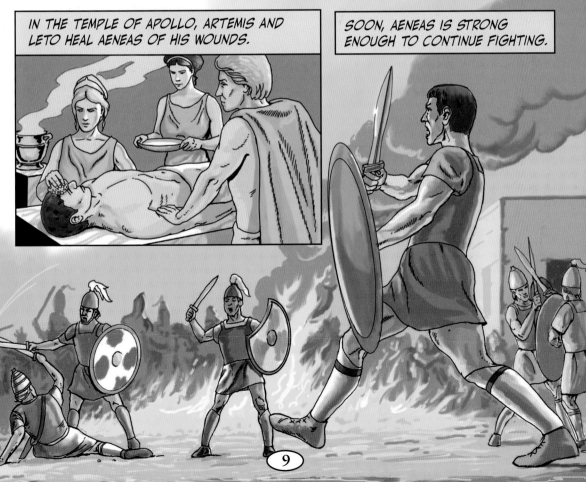

USING THE WOODEN TROJAN HORSE, THE GREEKS DEFEAT THE CITY OF TROY.

I WILL HOLD THEM BACK WHILE YOU ESCAPE!

AENEAS HELPS THE SURVIVORS ESCAPE.

SEEING HE CAN DO NO MORE, AENEAS LEAVES TROY CARRYING HIS FATHER ON HIS BACK.

LET HIM GO. HE IS HELPING AN OLD MAN.

FOR A WHILE, AENEAS STAYS AT MOUNT IDA, NEAR TROY, WITH HIS FELLOW TROJANS. BUT HE KNOWS THE GREEKS WILL NOT LET THEM STAY THERE FOREVER.

MY LORD, THE GREEKS ARE HUNTING DOWN THE SURVIVORS!

IT WON'T BE LONG BEFORE THEY FIND US HERE.

SEND A MESSENGER TO THE GREEKS TELLING THEM WE WILL LEAVE THIS LAND FOR GOOD IF THEY LET US GO PEACEFULLY.

THE GREEKS AGREE. WITH A FLEET OF TWENTY SHIPS, AENEAS AND HIS FOLLOWERS DEPART IN SEARCH OF A NEW PLACE TO SETTLE.

DO NOT WORRY. THE GODS WILL PROTECT US. THEY WILL SHOW US THE WAY TO THE PROMISED LAND WHERE WE WILL BUILD A NEW CITY.

THE FIRST STOP ON THEIR VOYAGE IS THRACE. SUDDENLY, A GHOST APPEARS BEFORE AENEAS!

GET AWAY FROM THIS CRUEL LAND!

WHO ARE YOU?

I AM POLYDORUS. KING OF THRACE. POLYMESTOR MURDERED ME. LEAVE THESE SHORES FOR YOUR OWN SAFETY.

AENEAS LEAVES THRACE AND SAILS ON TO CRETE. THE SHIPS DROP ANCHOR, AND AENEAS IS GREETED KINDLY BY KING ANIUS. HOWEVER THEY DO NOT STAY LONG.

WHY HAVE YOU CHOSEN THIS PLACE?

I THOUGHT THIS MIGHT BE THE PLACE FOR OUR NEW CITY, BUT I WAS WRONG. IT IS FULL OF DISEASE. WE MUST LEAVE IMMEDIATELY.

AS THEY LEAVE CRETE, THE GODS APPEAR BEFORE AENEAS.

...YOU MUST SAIL TO ITALY.

...SAIL TO ITALY.

...SAIL TO ITALY.

WHERE IS THIS ITALY?

GO TO BUTHROTUM. THERE YOU WILL FIND YOUR ANSWER.

YOU WILL NEVER FIND THE PLACE YOU SEEK. NOT UNTIL HUNGER FORCES YOU TO EAT THE TABLES YOUR FOOD IS ON!!!

ON THEIR WAY, THEY ARE ATTACKED BY WINGED MONSTERS - HARPIES.

13

IN BUTHROTUM, AENEAS IS GIVEN DIRECTIONS TO ITALY BY HELENUS. THEY SET OFF ONCE AGAIN BUT THE GODDESS, JUNO, SENDS A STORM THAT BLOWS THE SHIPS OFF COURSE...

THEY EVENTUALLY END UP AT A BEAUTIFUL CITY CALLED CARTHAGE IN NORTH AFRICA.

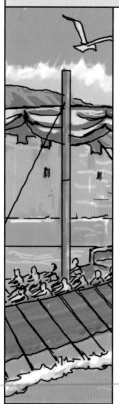

THIS CITY IS WONDERFUL!

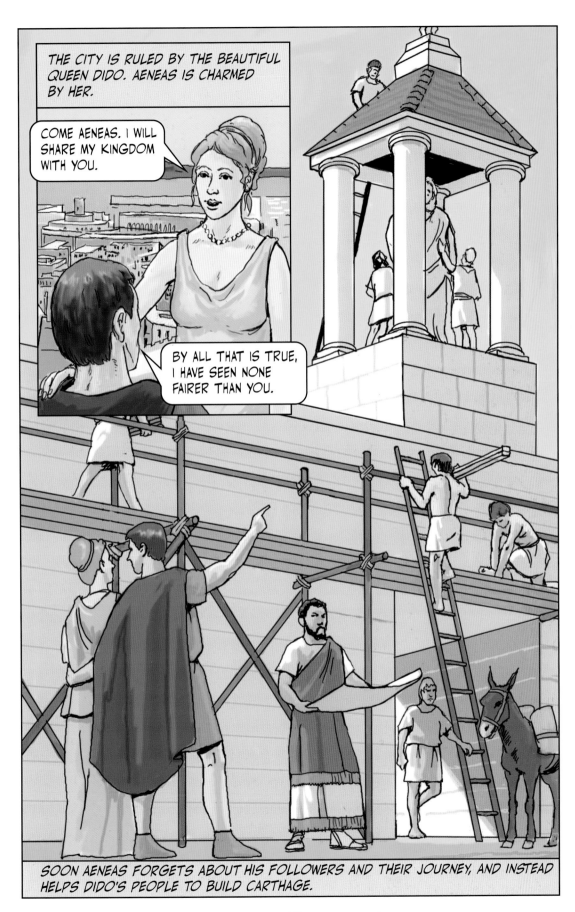

THE CITY IS RULED BY THE BEAUTIFUL QUEEN DIDO. AENEAS IS CHARMED BY HER.

COME AENEAS. I WILL SHARE MY KINGDOM WITH YOU.

BY ALL THAT IS TRUE, I HAVE SEEN NONE FAIRER THAN YOU.

SOON AENEAS FORGETS ABOUT HIS FOLLOWERS AND THEIR JOURNEY, AND INSTEAD HELPS DIDO'S PEOPLE TO BUILD CARTHAGE.

JUPITER, THE CHIEF GOD, WATCHES AENEAS AND CALLS FOR MERCURY, THE MESSENGER OF THE GODS.

HE HAS FORGOTTEN HIS QUEST. REMIND HIM OF HIS DESTINY!!!

NOW YOU ARE BUILDING CARTHAGE TO PLEASE A WOMAN? WHAT HAS HAPPENED TO YOUR JOURNEY?

YOU ARE RIGHT. I MUST LEAVE DIDO AND LEAD MY PEOPLE.

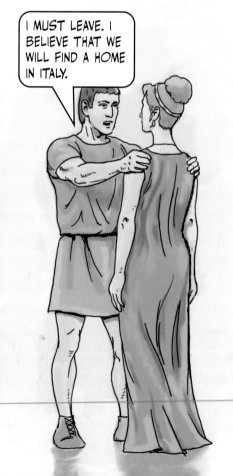

I MUST LEAVE. I BELIEVE THAT WE WILL FIND A HOME IN ITALY.

AENEAS GATHERS HIS FOLLOWERS FROM THE CITY AND SETS SAIL FOR ITALY.

17

DIDO CANNOT BEAR THE SEPARATION. IN HER GRIEF SHE FLINGS HERSELF INTO A FIRE AND DIES.

FROM HIS SHIP, AENEAS SEES A FIRE BURNING BRIGHTLY ON A TOWER HIGH ABOVE THE WALLS OF CARTHAGE.

FATHER, YOU LOOK ILL!

YES MY SON. I FEAR I AM NOT LONG FOR THIS WORLD.

BEFORE LONG, AENEAS' FATHER PEACEFULLY DIES. THE SHIPS STOP AT DREPANUM, SICILY, FOR ANCHISES' FUNERAL. HE IS BURIED AT THE FOOT OF A MOUNTAIN.

FROM NOW ON, LET THIS MOUNTAIN BE KNOWN AS ANCHISIA.

AFTER THE FUNERAL, AENEAS SETS SAIL ONCE MORE AND FINALLY LANDS ON THE ITALIAN COAST AT CUMAE. HERE HE SEARCHES FOR A GUIDE TO THE UNDERWORLD.

I AM TOLD THE SIBYL LIVES IN A CAVE NEAR HERE.

TELL ME, SIBYL, IS IT TRUE THAT THE GATE TO THE UNDERWORLD IS HERE?

I WISH TO SEE MY FATHER ONCE MORE.

I WILL TAKE YOU TO HIM.

BUT FIRST, YOU MUST PICK A GOLDEN BOUGH FROM THE SACRED GROVE TO LIGHT OUR WAY.

FINALLY THEY REACH THE SACRED MEADOWS OF ELYSIUM.

FATHER!

HUH?

BUT HIS FATHER IS A GHOST, AND AENEAS CANNOT EMBRACE HIM.

LET ME SHOW YOU THE FUTURE.

WHO ARE THEY?

THEY ARE CALLED THE ROMANS, AND THEY WILL CREATE A GREAT EMPIRE.

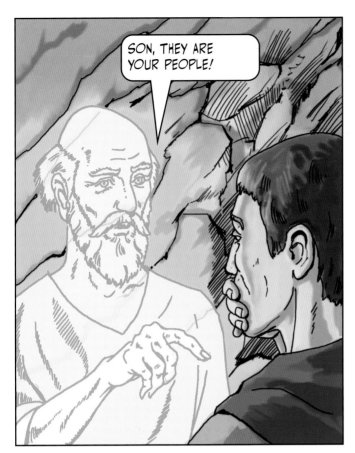

AENEAS AND THE SIBYL GO BACK THE WAY THEY CAME TO THE LAND OF THE LIVING...

THEIR SHIPS TRAVEL UP THE COAST AND STOP AT THE MOUTH OF THE RIVER TIBER.

LET'S GO ASHORE AND SET UP CAMP.

LATER, THEY ARE EATING THEIR MEAL OF MEAT ON SLICES OF WHEAT CAKE.

WHAT DID THE HARPIES SAY?

THAT WE WOULD ONLY FIND OUR HOME WHEN WE ATE THE TABLES OUR FOOD IS ON.

WELL, ARE WE NOT DOING JUST THAT?

YES, YOU'RE RIGHT. THIS WHEAT CAKE IS JUST LIKE A TABLE, AND THE MEAT IS FOOD ON TOP.

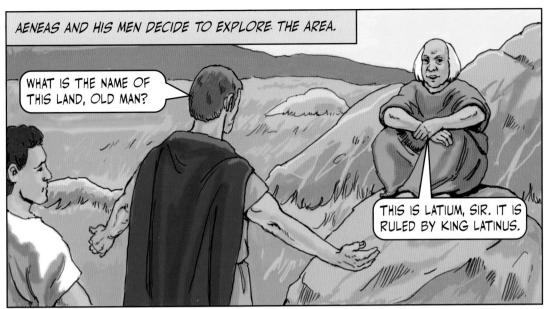

AENEAS AND HIS MEN DECIDE TO EXPLORE THE AREA.

WHAT IS THE NAME OF THIS LAND, OLD MAN?

THIS IS LATIUM, SIR. IT IS RULED BY KING LATINUS.

NEXT, AENEAS MEETS THE KING AND HIS DAUGHTER.

WE HAVE COME FROM TROY. I HAVE BEEN TOLD BY THE GODS TO BUILD A NEW CITY FOR MY PEOPLE.

YOU ARE WELCOME HERE, AENEAS. THERE ARE MANY PLACES TO BUILD A NEW CITY. BUT THERE ARE ALSO MANY TRIBES WHO WILL NOT TAKE KINDLY TO FOREIGNERS.

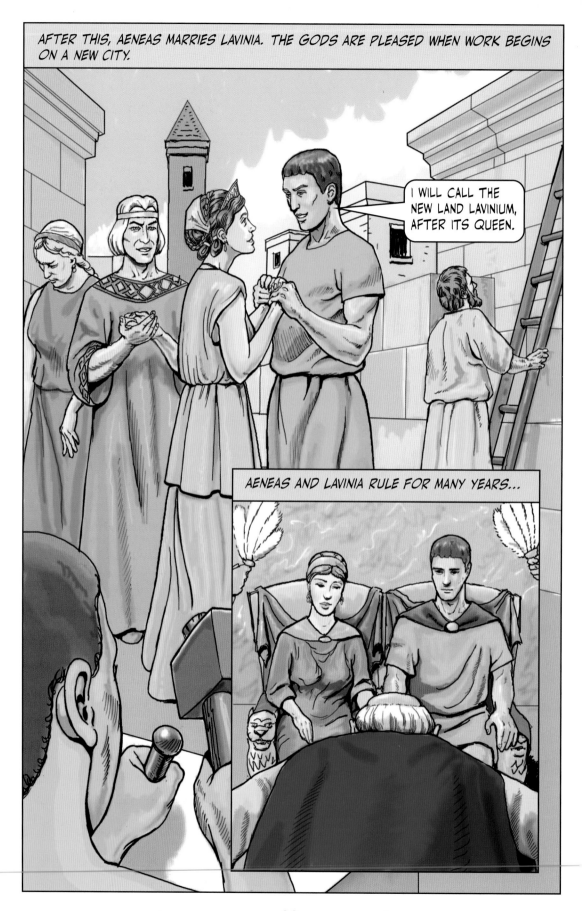

AFTER THIS, AENEAS MARRIES LAVINIA. THE GODS ARE PLEASED WHEN WORK BEGINS ON A NEW CITY.

I WILL CALL THE NEW LAND LAVINIUM, AFTER ITS QUEEN.

AENEAS AND LAVINIA RULE FOR MANY YEARS...

BUT THERE ARE ALWAYS ENEMIES TO FIGHT. SADLY, ONE DAY AENEAS IS KILLED IN A FIGHT WITH SOLDIERS OF MELENTIUS, AN OLD ALLY OF TURNUS'.

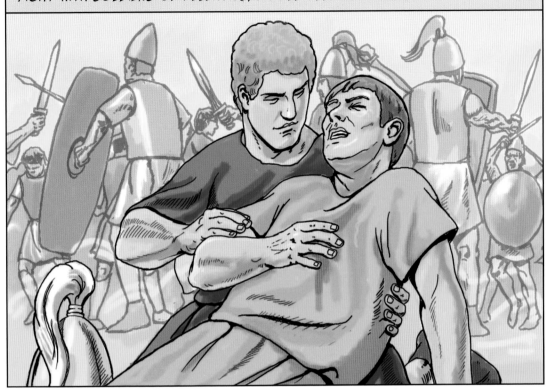

VENUS ASKS JUPITER TO MAKE AENEAS A GOD AND JUPITER GRANTS HER REQUEST.

YOU SHALL BE WORSHIPPED AS INDIGES.

THE END

ROMULUS AND REMUS

KING NUMITOR IS A RELATIVE OF AENEAS. HE IS THE RULER OF ALBA LONGA, A CITY FOUNDED BY AENEAS' SON.

KING NUMITOR HAS A BROTHER NAMED AMULIUS, WHO IS JEALOUS OF HIM.

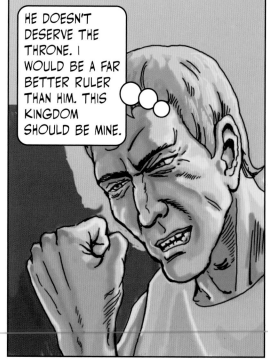

HE DOESN'T DESERVE THE THRONE. I WOULD BE A FAR BETTER RULER THAN HIM. THIS KINGDOM SHOULD BE MINE.

AMULIUS GATHERS HIS FOLLOWERS AND PLANS TO MURDER NUMITOR.

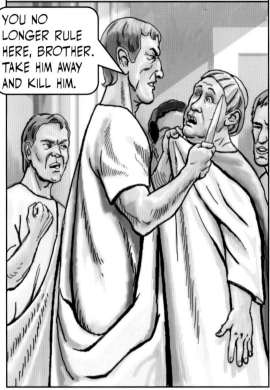

YOU NO LONGER RULE HERE, BROTHER. TAKE HIM AWAY AND KILL HIM.

NUMITOR MANAGES TO ESCAPE AND FLEES THE CITY.

AMULIUS IS NOW KING, BUT HE FEARS THAT HIS BROTHER'S GRANDSONS WILL ONE DAY TAKE THE THRONE FROM HIM. HE THINKS OF NUMITOR'S DAUGHTER, RHEA SILVIA.

HMM... SHE IS A WOMAN AND IS NO THREAT TO ME. BUT IF SHE WERE TO MARRY AND HAVE A SON...

TAKE HER TO THE TEMPLE OF VESTA.

ONCE SHE IS A PRIESTESS SHE WILL NOT BE ABLE TO MARRY.

HOWEVER, AMULIUS' PLAN IS RUINED. MARS, THE GOD OF WAR, SECRETLY VISITS RHEA SILVIA AND GIVES HER TWIN BOYS.

I SHALL CALL YOU ROMULUS. AND YOU SHALL BE REMUS.

WHAT?

TWINS?

BOYS?

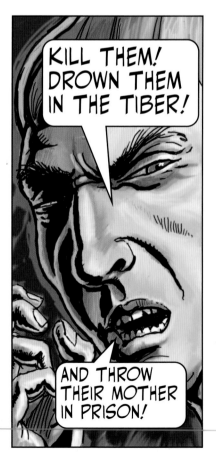

KILL THEM! DROWN THEM IN THE TIBER!

AND THROW THEIR MOTHER IN PRISON!

NOOOO!

NOT MY BABIES!

I'M SORRY, MY LADY, I'M ONLY FOLLOWING ORDERS.

THE SERVANT GIVEN THE TASK OF DROWNING THE TWINS TAKES PITY ON THEM.

I SHALL LET THE GODS DECIDE YOUR FATE.

THE BASKET COMES TO REST ON THE GENTLY SLOPING BANKS NEAR THE SEVEN HILLS.

WAAHH!

33

A SHE-WOLF, WHOSE CUBS HAVE JUST DIED...

...FINDS THE TWINS IN THE BASKET...

GRRR!

WAAH WAAH

SHE TAKES CARE OF THEM.

A FEW DAYS LATER, FAUSTULUS, A SHEPHERD, FINDS THE BOYS. HE TAKES THEM HOME AND RAISES THEM AS IF THEY WERE HIS OWN.

IN TIME, THE BOYS GROW UP TO BE STRONG AND HEALTHY. THEY ARE BOTH BRAVE YOUNG MEN.

ONE DAY...

FAUSTULUS, WHO WAS OUR MOTHER?

IT IS SAID YOU ARE THE SONS OF RHEA SILVIA.

AMULIUS TRIED TO HAVE YOU KILLED AND HE IMPRISONED YOUR MOTHER.

ONE DAY, WE WILL PUNISH AMULIUS FOR WHAT HE DID TO OUR MOTHER.

WHEN THEY ARE GROWN MEN, THE TWINS FORM A SMALL ARMY. THEY HAVE NEVER FORGOTTEN THEIR MOTHER'S SUFFERING – THEY ATTACK ALBA LONGA.

AMULIUS IS KILLED!!!

AAARGH!

RELEASE OUR MOTHER FROM PRISON NOW!

THE TWINS RESTORE NUMITOR TO THE THRONE OF ALBA LONGA, AND ONCE AGAIN, ORDER IS RESTORED.

ONE DAY, THE TWINS ARE WALKING NEAR THE SEVEN HILLS...

LET'S BUILD A CITY ON ONE OF THESE HILLS.

YES, BUT WHICH ONE?

THAT ONE IS THE OBVIOUS CHOICE.

I DISAGREE. THE ONE ON THE LEFT HAS HIGHER SLOPES!

ONLY ONE OF US CAN CHOOSE. TO DECIDE, I SUGGEST WE COUNT THE VULTURES WE SEE. THE ONE WITH THE MOST SIGHTINGS WINS.

VERY WELL.

AT THE END OF THE DAY, REMUS SAYS HE HAS SEEN SIX VULTURES.

HA! I HAVE SEEN TWELVE. SO, I CHOOSE THE HILL.

TWELVE? I DON'T BELIEVE YOU.

HORATIUS AND THE BRIDGE

IN 510 BC, THE ROMANS EXPELLED KING TARQUIN THE PROUD. LARS PORSENA, THE ETRUSCAN LEADER, DECIDED TO MAKE ROME PAY FOR THIS INSULT. HE GATHERED AN ARMY OF 90,000 MEN AND MARCHED ON ROME SEEKING REVENGE.

HORATIUS COCLES IS ON GUARD DUTY AT THE BRIDGE OVER THE TIBER. SUDDENLY, THE ETRUSCANS APPEAR ON THE JANICULUM HILL OPPOSITE...

IF THEY CAPTURE THIS BRIDGE, ROME WILL BE LOST.

THE ROMANS STREAM OVER THE BRIDGE, RUNNING FROM THE INVADERS.

IN HEAVEN'S NAME, STAND AND FIGHT!!!

BUT NO ONE STOPS... THEN HORATIUS REALISES HE MUST DO SOMETHING.

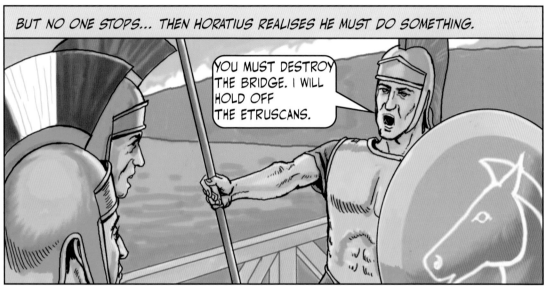

YOU MUST DESTROY THE BRIDGE. I WILL HOLD OFF THE ETRUSCANS.

TWO SOLDIERS – SPURIUS LARTIUS AND TITUS HERMINIUS – FEEL ASHAMED AT THE THOUGHT OF LETTING HORATIUS FACE THE ENEMY ALONE.

WE WILL JOIN YOU, HORATIUS.

THE THREE ROMANS STRUGGLE AGAINST THE HUGE ETRUSCAN ARMY. BUT THEY MANAGE TO STOP THE INVADERS ADVANCE.

THE FIGHTING IS FIERCE. BODIES BEGIN TO PILE UP IN FRONT OF THE THREE MEN.

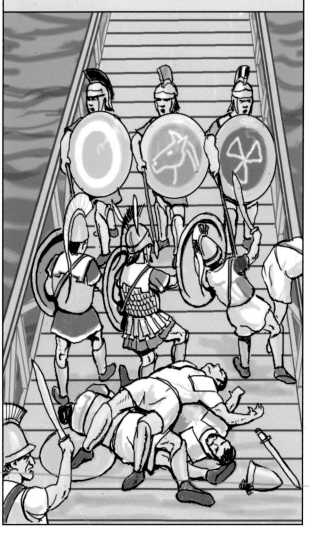

WHEN ONLY A SMALL PART OF THE BRIDGE IS LEFT, SPURIUS AND TITUS RUN BACK TO THE OTHER SIDE.

WHERE IS HORATIUS?

HE IS STILL FIGHTING.

SUDDENLY, THE REST OF THE BRIDGE COLLAPSES!!! HORATIUS IS TRAPPED ON THE WRONG SIDE!!!

KERRRACK

HORATIUS PRAYS TO THE RIVER GOD...

TIBERNIUS, HOLY FATHER, I PRAY THAT YOU WILL TAKE THIS ARMOUR AND THIS WARRIOR INTO YOUR STREAM.

HE DIVES INTO THE RIVER WEARING HIS HEAVY ARMOUR.

MIRACULOUSLY, HE SURFACES AND SWIMS FOR THE BANK.

HURRAH!

HURRAH!

HURRAH!

THUS, ROME IS SAVED. FOR HIS BRAVE DEEDS, HORATIUS IS REWARDED WITH LAND AND A STATUE OF HIM IS BUILT IN ROME.

HORATIUS COCLES

THE END

MORE MYTHICAL CHARACTERS

Most of the Roman gods and myths were borrowed from the ancient Greeks after the Romans conquered them in the second century BC. However, there were many characters from myths and legends that only appeared in Roman stories.

BELLONA – A goddess of war.

FAUNA – The wife of Faunus who was worshipped as the goddess of the fields and earth.

FAUNUS – The grandson of Saturn who was worshipped as the god of fields and shepherds. He was also the god of fortune-telling. He had the head and body of a man, and the legs of a goat.

FLORA – The goddess of flowers. She was always youthful and there was a festival to honour her in the spring and to pray for a good harvest.

GENIUS – A man's guardian spirit. The Romans believed that every man had his own Genius who would protect him throughout his life. On their birthdays, men gave presents to their Genius'.

JANUS – The porter of heaven and the month January is named after him. He is the guardian of gates and is shown as having two heads because every doorway faces two ways. There were many temples in Rome built for worshipping Janus.

JUNO – A woman's guardian spirit. Juno is the female version of the Genius – the spirit believed to protect Romans throughout their lives.

LARES – These were household gods. They were believed to be the souls of the dead ancestors who watched over and protected the living members.

LUCINA – The goddess of childbirth.

MITHRAS – A Persian god who was popular with Romans after they conquered the eastern Mediterranean. Mithras is often shown killing a bull with an axe.

PALES – The goddess of cows and fields.

PENATES – Household gods. Their name comes from the Roman word for pantry (where food was kept). Every home had a master who was the priest of the Penates.

POMONA – A goddess who looked after fruit trees.

QUIRINUS – A war god. He was said to be Romulus, founder of Rome, who was made a god after his death.

SATURN – An ancient Italian god. Some say that he was the Greek god Cronos, who was sent away from heaven by Jupiter, and went to Italy. The feast of Saturnalia was held every year in the winter. At the feast, no work was done and friends gave presents to each other. Slaves sat at their own table and were served by their masters. This showed that all people equal in Saturn's world.

TERMINUS – The god of landmarks. His statues were rough stones or posts, set in the ground to mark a boundary or end of a field.

VESTA – The goddess of the hearth (fireplace). A holy fire was kept alight in her temple by six pure priestesses called vestals.

GLOSSARY

ancestors Members of your family who lived a very long time ago.

bough A large branch from a tree.

conquer To defeat and triumph over an enemy.

destiny Things that will happen in the future that are beyond control.

Etruscans A civilisation that ruled most of Italy before the Romans.

expelled Being officially sent away from a place as a punishment.

grief Deep suffering, often after the death of a loved one.

grove A small group of trees.

harpies Vicious winged monsters with the heads and bodies of women, and the tails, wings, and claws of a bird.

incense A material that is burned to make a strong, pleasant smell.

oracle Someone who is considered to be very wise and can predict the future. An oracle can also talk with the gods.

Persians People from the country of Persia, in modern-day Iran.

Polydorus Youngest son of Hecuba and Priam, king of Troy. He was murdered by Polymestor, king of Thrace.

priestess A holy woman who oversees religious ceremonies.

prophetess A woman who can see into the future.

quest A search for something.

River Styx The main river in the underworld.

sacred When something is set apart as religious or holy.

Sibyl The prophetess who helps Aeneas on his journey to the underworld.

siege When an army surrounds a city and does not allow in supplies of food or water until the city surrenders..

superstitious A fear of the unknown or of religion or magic.

Trojan horse A huge wooden horse left as a gift for Troy by the Greeks. It was a trick, and when the Trojans brought it inside the gates, the Greeks hiding inside leapt out and defeated the city. This was how the Trojan war finally ended.

underworld The world of the dead, which is underneath the world of the living.

vultures Large birds of prey that feed on the bodies of dead animals.

worship Ceremonies and prayers dedicated to a god or gods.

FOR MORE INFORMATION

ORGANISATIONS

The British Museum
Great Russell Street
London
WC1B 3DG
www.thebritishmuseum.ac.uk

Ashmolean Museum of Art and Archaeology
Beaumont Street
Oxford
OX1 2PH
www.ashmol.ox.ac.uk

FOR FURTHER READING

If you liked this book, you might also want to try:

Roman Mythology
by Evelyn Wolfson, Enslow Publishers 2002

Inside Ancient Rome
by David Stewart, Book House 2005

Julius Caesar: The Life of a Roman General
by Gary Jeffrey and Kate Petty, Book House 2005

Graphic Myths: Greek
by Rob Shone, Book House 2006

The Roman Twins
by Roy Gerrard, Farrar Strauss Giroux 1999

INDEX

Websites
Due to the changing nature of Internet links, the Salariya Book Company has developed an online list of Web sites related to the subject of this book. This site is updated regularly. Please use this link to access the list:
http://www.book-house.co.uk/gmyth/roman